OXFORD'S
GARGOYLES
AND
GROTESQUES

John Blackwood

Photographs by
David Collett

Charon Press 1986

Introduction

As you cross Magdalen Bridge and enter Oxford from the east, you receive a blessing; from the first corner on the right there emerges an episcopal figure, his hand raised in benediction (1). From a cathedral city and from a university founded by churchmen, such a welcome might be expected. But if you look closely along the building — for the first time, perhaps, though you may often have passed this way before — you will see that the stonework is peopled with carved figures: a winged lion, a man riding a horned demon, and faces, staring and soulful. If then, from a suitable vantage, you look up at Magdalen Tower, you will see, upon the battlements and pinnacles, mermaids (4) and demons, wrestlers and woodmen, horses and frogs. All these figures seem perfectly at home; no one questions their right to be there. Yet why should such motley clothe a Christian edifice? And what have a pair of lovers in eternal embrace or a weather-beaten harvester (2) to do with the pursuit of academic excellence?

The answer takes us back to the Middle Ages. From the twelfth century on, it became the custom to decorate churches and cathedrals with carvings of an extraordinary diversity and inventiveness. These figures often had a grotesque character; they were full of humour and horror — humour fraught with horror and horror tempered with humour. Demons and dragons appeared in great numbers, seeming to guard the buildings of the very religion which had subdued them.

Not every churchman approved of what was happening. In 1125 St. Bernard of Clairvaux complained to a fellow abbot, "Of what use to the brothers reading piously in the cloisters are these ridiculous monstrosities, these prodigies of deformed beauty, these beautiful deformities? . . . There on one body grow several heads, and several heads have one body; here a quadruped wears the head of a serpent and the head of a quadruped appears on the body of a fish . . . Almighty God! If we are not ashamed of these unclean things, we should at least regret what we have spent on them." A controversy ensued between St. Bernard's Cistercian order and the Benedictines of Cluny. One of the more ingenious arguments employed by the latter ran as follows: God is beyond description of any kind and these grotesque carvings, by stretching our imaginations to their limits, remind us of this. St. Bernard clearly had little sense of humour; others argued that humour, being natural to man, had its rightful place in the worship of God, especially since the Church had a duty to minister to the simple and illiterate as well as to the learned. Certainly, to the mediaeval mind, all kinds of symbolic relationship were possible. A pair of lovers might represent the marriage of reason and revelation, and a harvester with a sickle was obviously both Time and He who would come at time's end to bind up the wheat and the tares.

While the monks debated, the carvers carved. What they themselves thought of what they were doing, they did not tell us; they worked with stone, not words. Perhaps they were just enjoying themselves (3). Certainly it was the Church which offered them the best prospect of employment and of advancement to an established place in society.

Oxford University has its roots in mediaeval Christianity. Its oldest surviving colleges date from the thirteenth and fourteenth centuries and were founded to improve the learning of the clergy. The quadrangle, that essential feature of college architecture, doubtless evolved from the monastic cloister and several colleges have cloisters of their own. It was therefore natural that from their earliest days college buildings should have been decorated with grotesque carvings in the mediaeval Gothic manner. This style lasted longer in conservative Oxford than anywhere else in England; Canterbury Quad in St. John's College, built in 1631–6, is part Gothic and has a great number of carved figures. During subsequent centuries the

1 Bishop Waynflete, founder of Magdalen College, blesses you as you enter Oxford from the east.

2 A harvester occupies a corner further along the same building. Is he also Time, the reaper?

3

3 Carvers, it seems, have always enjoyed poking fun at musicians, especially pipers, who soundlessly puff out their cheeks and entangle themselves with their instruments. This piper is on Magdalen's St. Swithun's building, further up the High Street.

4 A mermaid on the west side of Magdalen Tower has the enchanting face of one of the maids in the college buttery.

4

architectural heart of the city remained more or less intact and the carver's art continued to find expression, particularly during the Gothic revival of the second half of the nineteenth century. Now, over the last thirty years, Oxford's buildings have undergone an unparallelled programme of restoration, and this has attracted gifted carvers to live and work here.

There are in Oxford hundreds, if not thousands, of these strange and remarkable carvings. This book provides an introduction to them, tracing a circular route through the city. The journey, mapped on the last page of the book, begins at the Bodleian Library, crosses Radcliffe Square, proceeds to Merton College, Magdalen College, then down Queen's Lane to St. Edmund Hall and New College, returning once more to the famous heads around the Sheldonian Theatre. From there further possibilities present themselves. As the tour proceeds, the subject gradually unfolds. If you prefer, you can make the journey from the comfort of your armchair, using the photographs provided. On foot, you will certainly find that the full tour will take you more than a day. You should aim to travel in the afternoon, since the majority of the colleges are open to visitors only between 2 and 5 or 6 pm. After Merton, a diversion from the main route to Christ Church is suggested as a way of breaking the tour half way. Some highlights have been reserved for the second half of the circle: if you only have time for one quick tour of two hours or so, you should begin with the full explanation of the Sheldonian heads found later in the book and then proceed in reverse order to New College, St. Edmund Hall and Magdalen. Of course if you live in Oxford you can use the book for a leisurely discovery lasting weeks, months or years. A pair of binoculars is a great help in revealing the detail of the more distant figures. There is much to see. You should go at your own pace and find your own friends and favourites; a guide can only point the way. Once you know the carvings are there, you will find them everywhere.

The Bodleian Library

Our tour begins at the south east end of Broad street, opposite Blackwell's bookshop and beneath Oxford's most conspicuous carved heads, the ring of "Emperors" or "Philosophers" surrounding the Sheldonian Theatre. They are in fact neither of these; they are guardians, gods of ends and beginnings. Their full history will be described later. For now, allow them to admit you into a new and mysterious world of vision. If it is a weekday, or a Saturday morning, the little wooden door beneath the right hand end of the ring of heads will be open; go through it and around the right hand side of the Sheldonian. Facing you will be the Duke Humphrey Library, completed at the end of the fifteenth century. (If the door is closed, skip the rest of this paragraph, follow the ring of heads to the left and turn to the right down Catte Street, where the rest of the Bodleian Library will come into view). High up, under the battlements, is a line of carvings of a highly fantastical nature. Among the figures immediately above you is a frog swallowing a fly, and a pair of salamanders with faces like roses (in mediaeval alchemy, the salamander represented the inner fire of transformation and the rose the rubedo or reddening which marked the completion of the work). Monstrous heads glower down; around the first corner there is a snake-haired Medusa, herself most unhappily petrified. Choirs of angels (3) and demons (4) are ranged opposite each other within the central buttresses. On your left is a cheery fellow all face and arms (1). The rest are a mediaeval bestiary; there is the peacock whose flesh does not decay, the dolphin whose coming portends storms and many others.

1 This sprightly gentleman — a stone spirit, or lapid one might call him — seems to be emerging from the wall.

2 A soldier, his face darkened by the sun of many campaigns (and partial cleaning). Behind his back, a bumpkin derides both him and us.

5 Dwarves locked in eyeball confrontation over possession of a nugget of gold, or the deadline for the next delivery of swords. More subterranean counterpoint here: phallic creatures enclosing a fallopian space.

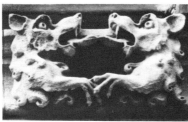

6 No hostility between these heraldic beasts, their hands and tongues most touchingly joined.

3 & 4 A choir of angels confronts a similar company of demons. They keep up their counterpoint from the corners of the central buttresses of the Duke Humphrey Library.

Continuing on, you come to the outer, north wall of the Schools Quadrangle, built in the early seventeenth century under the auspices of Sir Thomas Bodley; the letters TB are his monogram. The carvings here are on the whole gentler and simpler in style. There are these quarrelling dwarves (5), an elf who might have come from the pages of *A Midsummer Night's Dream*, a dog chasing a rabbit. There are many human heads, some of them more resembling theatrical masks. As you go through the ironwork gate and turn right down Catte Street, along the east side of the library, look especially at the heads above the window over the main gateway. Here is a helmeted soldier and his discourteous neighbour (2), and on the other side of the window are lawyer and laughter. High above, on the left side, a dragon is whispering unwelcome news into someone's ear — or is he biting the ear off?

And now we must prepare you for, perhaps, a small shock of disillusionment. The carvings are not mediaeval or seventeenth century; they are in fact just about thirty years old. During the late 1950's the Bodleian Library was restored as part of the Oxford Historic Buildings Fund programme and the carvings, most of which had become little more than vague shapes, were replaced. However, a carving is not less to be admired because it is not old or original; what matters is its quality and appropriateness. The Bodleian carvings were done at Bradfords Ltd., who were one of the last of the once numerous London masonary companies specialising in this kind of traditional work. Some of their carvers came from carving families. All had served apprenticeships during which they learned the techniques of their craft and its repetoire of designs. Bradfords' foreman carver was then Mr Kenneth Gardner, who later took charge of the carving at St. Paul's Cathedral. John Love-Symonds, Reg Parnell and Adam Bienkowski also carved work for the Bodleian Library, and should not be allowed to pass into the customary oblivion. Researching and supervising the designs were Mr A. W. Banks, managing director of Bradfords, and Mr R. J. Potter, the architect in charge of the restoration.

On the south outer wall, basking in the midday sun, are these loving creatures (6). Further along you will find the angel of the sun himself. There are many more carvings inside the Schools Quadrangle, some grotesque, some, of learned men past and present, of a more conventional kind. However, there is much to see; you should perhaps leave these for another day and make your way across Radcliffe Square to the University Church of St. Mary the Virgin.

The Church of St. Mary the Virgin

High up on the University Church are the first true gargoyles of the tour. A gargoyle has a function; it takes the rain from the guttering behind it, "gargling" it and spewing it out through its mouth. (The word comes from its French equivalent *gargouille*, which in old French also meant throat. Gargouille was likewise the name given to the ravaging dragon subdued by St. Romanus, first bishop of Rouen). This means of drainage was used occasionally in the ancient world; there were lion-headed gargoyles at Pompeii. It was rediscovered and began to be used extensively in the thirteenth century. If rain is allowed to run unchecked down walls, it produces damp, discolouration and decay. The previous, not very satisfactory solution had been simply to allow the water to drip from overhanging eaves. Long cast-iron pipes were beyond the skills of mediaeval metal-workers, though gargoyles were sometimes given short iron or lead pipes which protruded from their mouths.

The St. Mary's gargoyles are a mixed company of winged beasts and cowled human figures projecting from around the base of the spire (1). If you climb up to the tower gallery, you can see clearly how the water from it runs along open channels grooved in the gargoyles' backs and out through their mouths — so long as these have not been choked with earth. Clearly, people regard them with veneration, treating them as wishing wells, since the channels are full of coins. Above the gallery, around the saints in their niches, more creatures cluster, aerial guardians forever poised to launch themselves in flight. Most have the wings of angels, a few the ribbed,

1 One of the gargoyles around the base of St. Mary's spire, a nun bewailing the world's sins and sorrows.

2 This lion-man is also a true gargoyle; the water runs from the guttering behind him and out through the pipe in his mouth.

3 A Magdalen College monkey, also passing water?

1

bat-like wings more appropriate to demons.

St. Mary's spire was built between 1315 and 1325, but its carvings are much more recent; they date from Sir Thomas Jackson's restoration of 1892–6. They are in fact in good repair for their near hundred years. This is because T.G. "Oxford" Jackson, architect of the Examination Schools and many other University buildings, also had the distinction of introducing Clipsham stone to the city. This is a limestone from Rutland and much more durable than the limestones used previously; these came from local quarries at Headington or Wheatley, from Taynton and Barrington near Burford on the edge of the Cotswolds or, latterly, from Bath. Exposed to wind and weather and to the soot from the fires which all undergraduates used to have burning in their rooms, the older stonework peeled and cracked. The carvings, being the most exposed, wore away fastest; many of the figures which Jackson replaced had been carved in Taynton stone at the previous restoration and had completely decayed though put up only forty years before. Jackson's restoration came about because of a most dramatic and dangerous event; one windy March morning, the head of an archbishop in one of the tower niches fell and embedded itself in the ground by the north door, very shortly after the entry of the Vice Chancellor who was attending the University sermon.

Halfway up to the gallery, from the metal ladder leading up to the bell loft, you get a close-up view of some of the many pinnacles which spring from the roof-line in this part of Oxford like the trees of a forest. They are ornamented with curly whirls of stone called crockets, the lowest four of which are always grotesque creatures. From the ladder you can also see the carvings along the top of the north side of the main nave. Immediately facing you is this ass (5); it is in fact Balaam's ass, shying away from the angel blocking its path. Balaam (4) is further along the same line of figures and must be seen from the ground. The two were part of a planned Old Testament series which was unfortunately never completed.

Next to Balaam is a gargoyle lion-man chewing on his lead pipe (2). There are, indeed, very few true gargoyles left in Oxford since the modern drainpipe took over. For example, according to Loggan's 1675 engraving the High Street front of All Soul's College, which you will shortly see, had no less than eleven gargoyles whose pipes dripped water onto the heads of the passers-by; now there are none. There are, however, in a number of places, what might be called hybrids, figures which take the water from the guttering and pass it into the head of a drainpipe beneath. You see one of these figures as you take the passageway on the left of St. Mary's by which Catte Street joins the High Street. The finest drainheads in Oxford are those in Canterbury Quad, St. John's College — not on our main route but well worth a visit. This Magdalen College monkey is assuming a quasi-functional attitude above his drainhead (3). If you should think him in poor taste, you should remember that an element of the vulgar was traditional in this kind of carving.

4 & 5 The prophet Balaam went on a journey displeasing to God and was turned back by an angel. His cagey ass can see the angel; the indignant Balaam, as yet, cannot. Shortly, goaded by Balaam's blows, the ass will turn and utter human speech.

8

1

1 Arcady in Academe. Pan, from his high corner, pipes to All Souls across the level lawns.

2 This musician proudly displays his instrument, a mediaeval double pipe.

3 Cheeks puffed out, this horn player is in full cry.

All Souls

The figures on the outside of All Souls, which you now see, are the work of Mr. E. S. Frith, for many years one of Oxford's senior carvers, a Victorian gentleman in the twentieth century. He also did the Canterbury Quad figures, with the assistance of Mr. Michael Black, the carver of the Sheldonian heads, who trained with him.

The newer carvings inside the Front Quad of All Souls are particularly fine. One of my own favourites is the musician whom you see immediately on your right (2). He is holding a late mediaeval double pipe, the original of which was dug up in 1896 when the College was enlarging its smoking room; it is now exhibited in the Bate collection in the Music Faculty building in St. Aldates. It is the only one in existence and the College, being justly proud of it, requested its commemoration in stone. Other echoes inhabit the quad: bucolic, like those of this horn (3), and ancient — for in the far right hand corner the oldest god of all, Pan, is playing his pipes (1).

None of these figures, as you can see, can properly be called gargoyles; there are some amusing faces over the drainpipes, but no true waterspouts. Because of their exaggerated forms and expressions, the generally accepted term for them is grotesques. The Middle Ages called them babewyns, from the Italian word *babunio* meaning baboon. Chaucer, in his *House of Fame*, speaks of "babewynnes and pinacles, imageries and tabernacles." The word meant any sort of humorous, fantastic decoration, whether carved, embroidered on a robe or drawn on an illuminated manuscript. Monkeys were often used in these decorations; the ape loves to imitate man and thus provides an ideal vehicle for humorous mockery. The term is a nice one and it would be good to see it back in use. Now, as you look up at the tower above the front gateway, you will see on its left hand corner a babewyn carving its own babewyn (4).

In the centre of the tower is the head of King Henry VI, one of the co-founders of the college. According to historical records his left ear was unnaturally small, and so it is here. The creator of these All Souls figures, and of Balaam and his ass, is Mr. Michael Groser, surely one of the finest carvers of babewyns in the country. He has lived and worked in Oxford since 1955; you will be seeing the greatest range of his work at New College.

2

3

St. Mary's: High Street Front

4 A babewyn apes his creator with mallet and chisel.

From the Front Quad of All Souls you get a fine, open view of the east side of St. Mary's spire (especially if you have a pair of binoculars to help you distinguish the detail). Around the saint on the left hand, south east corner, instead of the usual beasts, are three armed men, one with shield and sword and another in a coat of mail. Jackson copied these from existing figures without knowing their exact purpose; the saint may be Thomas à Beckett and the armed men his murderers.

 Almost everything you have seen so far has been in such an unspoiled state that it is hard to imagine what was there before. But as you return up the High Street, look at the lower set of carvings on St. Mary's, level with the top of the porch. Here, as yet unreplaced, are things "wounded, broken, sloughing off their outer shape in the deadly struggle against years, weather and man." The quotation is from Thomas Hardy's novel *Jude the Obscure*, for it is as a stone carver that its hero, the village orphan Jude Fawley, comes to Christminster, Hardy's name for Oxford. Jude works restoring the University's buildings; he longs to enter its charmed world of learning, but it rejects his homespun aspirations. On his first evening in the city he wanders down ancient alleys, past walls and doorways, feeling their contours with his fingers. "Their extinct air," Hardy reflects, "was accentuated by the rottenness of their stones." You can get a flavour of this as you turn briefly down the narrow passageway which runs along the west side of St. Mary's. The heroine of the novel, Sue Bridehead, would in her free-thinking days have rejoiced to catch sight of the golden Pans carved each side of a doorway here (5). For having statues of Venus and Apollo in her room, she was expelled by her pious Christminster landlady. Throughout the book, the Christian Gothic symbolises the outworn ways of thought and social convention which end by destroying both her and Jude.

5 This golden satyr, crouched in the angle of a doorway, surprises. What exactly is his expression: all seeing, unseeing, ecstatic or ruminant?

1 How many foolish creatures are there here! How humorous mankind is!

2 Not even dons escape the jester's eye.

Overleaf

3 A friar leans down from a window jamb and idly picks his nose.

4 A well dressed man gives vent to his disgust. Has he eaten, or seen, too much?

5 Masons like these prepared the stones which you are looking at and fixed them into place.

6 Plumbers made the pipes, and hard work it was, too. One of these plumbers is shaping a lead pipe; the ladle is for pouring the metal when it is molten.

7 These conspiratorial twins are carpenters (or possibly masons) sawing and chiselling at the same block.

Brasenose: High Street Front.

How differently did those other men of letters, John Ruskin and William Morris, feel. Both saw in the building of the mediaeval cathedrals an ideal, organic unity in which architect and artisan, designer and producer, were one and the same, and when comparatively unselfconscious craftsmen produced living and vital work. Both men left their mark on Oxford. Morris, as an undergraduate, assisted Rossetti and others in painting the Arthurian murals in the Union Library. Ruskin was Oxford's first Slade Professor of Art and one of the chief inspirers of the University Museum which has an important place on our tour. In "The Stones Of Venice" he pondered long on the meaning of the grotesque: the ludicrous and the fearful, the sportive and the terrible. One of the ideas which he explored is that the grotesque manner enables the artist to approach, through play and irony, matters which he would be unable to confront directly. In other words some of these apparently humourous carvings may be expressing things that would otherwise be too terrible to recognise.

Both Ruskin and William Morris had a great influence on their time. Sir Thomas Jackson, whom we have already met, was a friend of Morris and a member of the Arts and Crafts Society which he founded. He shared his views on the mediaeval period, looking back to "those happy days before professionalism had taken the architect from the building-shed and scaffolding and set him on a stool in an office, driving painting and sculpture from the walls of buildings to the studio and gallery." Morris put his ideas into practice by becoming skilled in a great number of crafts and by marketing many of his rich and beautiful creations. Jackson, too, was a gifted artist and stone-carver and so produced excellent designs for those who worked for him. Chief among these was a Mr. Maples, his principal carver for twenty years.

All this you will find reflected in the next set of figures which come to view. These are on the High Street from of Brasenose College, next to St. Mary's. To get the best view of them, you should cross to the other side of the street. Jackson designed the building, which was erected between 1891 and 1899. His views on the importance of spontaneity and the dignity of labour are surely reflected in the most outstanding of the carvings — the five drainhead panels which show various workmen: a mason with his hammer, masons fixing a stone (5), plumbers with pipe and ladle (6), carpenters (7) and a bricklayer. There are also expressive dragons and richly comical heads (1, 3, 4), including a somewhat motheaten don in a mortar board (2). Note the amazing variety of headress, caps, wimples and scarves. Gestures, too, are their speciality; they scratch their eyes, cheeks, noses and mouths, they suffer headache and toothache. On the tower above are caricatures of a rugby player holding the ball under his right arm and, on the left side of the tower, a 'cellist. The carvings have a wonderful life, with none of the stiffness of some of the work of the Victorian Gothic Revival.

Brasenose is, of course, named after a grotesque — the Brazen Nose, an ancient knocker of the kind once used to claim sanctuary in a sacred building. It has a sad, kind face, with dog-like ears, and it has sought its own sanctuary in the college dining-hall. Various stories are told about it. One is that it portrays the college's founder (though it was in fact in the possession of the hall of residence predating the college). Another is that offending undergraduates were obliged to sit upon its brassy prominence for two hours at a stretch, and that in this way it acquired its smooth and rounded form. One day you should pay it a visit and judge the truth of the story for yourself. For now, however, you should make your way back along the south side of the High Street and turn right down Magpie Lane, one of Oxford's many narrow and beautiful lanes, to Merton College.

3

4

5

6

1

Merton College

As you walk down Magpie Lane it is Merton chapel tower which first meets
your eye; beneath its battlements is a line of grotesques (3). As you turn left
into Merton Lane you see huge figures jutting out from the chapel's north
side, some one, some two-headed, some smiling, and some grimacing in
agony, struggling to escape from the stone in which they are imprisoned (2).
The originals of these figures date from the building of the chapel; they were
once fully functioning gargoyles, but in 1827 drainpipes were installed and
their mouths were concreted up. By the 1950's, worn stumps were all that
remained of them. In 1958 Merton began a thirty year restoration
programme, the company responsible for the work being Axtell, Perry and
Symm Masonry Ltd. They are Oxford's largest company of masons and
restorers, with offices and yards in Osney Mead. As Symm and Co. they
have been working on University buildings since the eighteenth century.
With the recent concentration of restoration work here in Oxford, they have
become one of the country's leading masons. Their work often takes
them to well-known places, for example the House of Commons. Axtell's
chief carver is Mr. Percy Quick, who was apprenticed in Liverpool and
came to Oxford in 1959. He made the replacements for the large chapel
figures, basing his designs on the existing shapes and on old drawings and
photographs, such as they were; this still left him considerable scope for
invention. He also carved the grotesques around the top of the tower, which
are well calculated to impress the eye at the distance from which they are
seen. There are other, smaller carvings to be remarked on, among them the
frieze of heads beneath the large figures.

Above the entrance to Merton is a late fifteenth century plaque depicting a
woodland scene (1). The workmanship is exquisite — even the burrowing
creatures can be clearly seen — and the beings who inhabit it make it seem
like the forest of Broceliande of Arthurian romance. There is a lamb and a
unicorn; both are symbols of Christ, the latter since it could be apprehended
only after it had laid its head in the lap of a virgin. In the centre is a book and,
since it has seven seals, it may be the one in Revelations opened by the Lamb
of God. The mitred figure is likely to be Walter de Merton, who founded the
college and next to him St. John the Baptist to whom it is dedicated. Since its
installation during the Wardenship of Richard Fitzjames (1483–1501), parts
of the plaque have been replaced and it has been recently cleaned, but it

1 This beautiful woodland scene is set
over the gateway to Merton College. It
is possible to guess at the identity and
meaning of the personages, both human
and animal, but the overwhelming
impression is one of mystery.

2 One of the massive carvings
protruding from the north side of
Merton chapel. A cheery, tuniced
fellow — a carver perhaps — with a bad
tempered, bat winged alter ego
squatting on his head.

2

3 Grotesques on Merton chapel tower. Their most noticeable features are their ranked teeth and curling tongues.

standard3

remains essentially the same work. It finds a place on our tour not because it is in any way a grotesque, but because of its great strangeness.

It may also be strange to find in Merton a complete set of carvings representing the signs of the Zodiac. These are on the roof of the Fitzjames Arch, which is in the left, far corner of the Front Quadrangle. Eight of the signs are in a cicle and the cardinal signs of solstice and equinox, the Ram, the Crab, the Scales and the Goat are in a cross around them. They date from the same time as the gateway plaque, nearly two hundred years before astrology and astronomy parted company. The shell of the Crab had to be replaced during the current restoration, a task which earned its carver a free supper on top of his usual wages.

You reach the entrance to the chapel by wending your way through Mob Quad, the oldest quadrangle in Oxford. There are no corresponding giant gargoyles to be seen on this side, and this follows an arrangement often met with in mediaeval churches. Around the door on the warm, south side are often found angels welcoming in the believer; the evil in the soul, symbolised by flying demons, is expelled out through the walls on the cold north side. (The north door was sometimes called 'the devil's door'). There too is the graveyard — as it is at Merton — and this display of power serves to keep in order any spirits that might attempt to wander there.

The oldest of Merton's carvings are to be found inside the chapel, on the corbels (or supporting stones) at the base of the pillars along each side of the chancel. Protected from wind and rain, they have endured since the building of the chapel at the end of the thirteenth century. Some of these carvings are what are now known as Green Men: heads surrounded by leaves and by branches which sometimes emerge from their mouths. They were often used as decorations in mediaeval churches and cathedrals; there are Green Men at Lincoln, Norwich, Ely, Wells and Exeter. It may be that they symbolised the natural, fallen world in contrast to the unchanging heights of Heaven. They clearly show the continuity of nature, the branches emerging from and returning to the face. One thinks also of the mediaeval story in which the Tree of Life grew from seeds planted in Adam's mouth; from that tree came the wood which made Christ's cross.

It is difficult not to see in the Green Men a throwback to earlier rites, to some deity of the wood or to the sacrificial May King crowned with garlands. Joyful celebrations of the May continued to be centred on churches until well into Tudor and Stuart times. Philip Stubbes, in his Anatomy of Abuses (1583) gives a vivid if disapproving picture of what went on.

"Then march this heathen company towards the Church and Churchyard, their Pipers pipeing, their Drommers thondryng, their bells jingling, their hobbie horses and other monsters skirmishing among the route: and in this sort they go into the Church (though the Minister be at prayer or preaching) dauncing and swinging their handkerchiefs over their heads in the Church like Devilles incarnate." Amongst the "monsters" might well have been a man swathed but for his face in leaves and branches.

There are a number of these foliate heads in Oxford. The Merton ones have intricately patterned crowns. Some are on their sides; they seem asleep, dreaming their leafy worlds into existence (1). There are three such heads on the thirteenth century tomb of St. Frideswide in Christ Church Cathedral, the carving cut deep into stone of great hardness (2). The carvers who worked at Magdalen College produced some fine Green Men (4, 5) and there have been other, more modern versions of the theme, for example on the Wadham College gateway tower.

Interlude: Christ Church

If you have followed the tour so far, you may feel that you have seen almost enough for the day. A way of rounding off is to leave the main route and pay a visit to Christ Church, whose chapel is also the Cathedral of Oxford. This, with its cloisters and Chapter House, was previously part of the Augustinian Priory of St. Frideswide, dissolved at the time of the Reformation. Go down Merton Grove, past the west end of the chapel, then turn right along Broad Walk until you come to the Meadow Buildings' entrance to Christ Church. There ask to be directed to the cloisters. The Chapter House, which opens onto them, has a fine Norman Doorway carved in the traditional zig-zag manner. (If you want to see more Norman carving, you should go to Iffley on the eastern outskirts of the town; its church has some of the finest in the country. St. Ebbe's church in the centre of the town has a smaller Norman doorway decorated with beak heads, probably restored). Inside the Chapter House are some amusing and very well preserved heads on the corbels of the pillars. These were carved by John of Gloucester in 1225; here is one expressing himself in a traditional way (3). From the cloisters, now a Tudor garden, you can look up at Wolsey Tower over the entrance to the dining hall: its corner pinnacles alone have ten grotesques apiece. All this area has recently been restored by Axtell, Perry and Symm (p. 20, 1 & 2).

In the chapel is the tomb of St. Frideswide (2). The pillars of both nave and chancel have corbel heads which have the look of caricatures, though no one knows whom they might represent. As you come out of the chapel, notice the humorous grotesques above the dining hall to your left. If then you feel in need of refreshment after all you have seen, you may leave Christ Church by the front gate and take a well-earned cup of tea at St. Aldate's Bookshop.

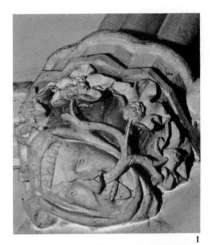

1

2

3

1 The most grotesque of the Merton chapel Green Men, for whom the dream has become something of a nightmare.

2 One of the three foliate heads on the tomb of St. Frideswide in Christ Church Cathedral. Perhaps they show the saint herself. If so, the choice of oak leaves is particularly appropriate, since the oak symbolises endurance and is the tree of Jove the wielder of lightning. Frideswide was the daughter of a Saxon king; she resolutely refused all offers of marriage and in answer to her prayers her final and most importunate suitor was struck down by a lightening bolt. The heads are on the oldest part of the reconstituted tomb.

3 One of the heads in Christ Church Chapter House. The tongue protrudes, but it is hard to say whether the gesture is comic or tragic. The three figures in the left hand column all belong to the thirteenth century and they and their fellows are therefore (with the exception of what is to be found on the various Norman doorways) Oxford's oldest surviving carvings.

4 & 5 Two of the Green Men on Magdalen's St. Swithun's building. One is surrounded by vine leaves and grapes, the other is of a most unusual design. During the nineteenth century, it was the chimney sweeps who dressed themselves in frames of leaves and flowers and, as Jack-of-the-Green, danced through the streets on May Morning begging for money. It is recorded that, after a long lapse, this custom reappeared in Oxford very shortly after the completion of the St. Swithun's building in 1882. Perhaps they were Magdalen sweeps inspired by the new carvings.

4

5

1

2

3

5

1 Mr R. T. Biscoe-Taylor on Magdalen Tower, attended by dragon and frog; he was surveyor-in-charge during its restoration.

2 Mr. Biscoe-Taylor on his way to attend to some dry rot in Tom Quad, Christ Church.

3 Two of the caricatures around the south-west corner of the tower, Messrs Quick and Hale.

4 Percy Quick, puts the finishing touches to the Tudor rose on a carved panel.

5 Mick Hale (now bearded) on site at New College.

6 Mr. Myles, managing director of Axtell, Perry and Symm Ltd, lionised by his chief carver.

7 Mr. Myles in his office in Osney Mead.

6

7

Magdalen College

The main tour continues along cobbled Merton Lane and down the High Street to Magdalen College, where you will find Oxford's most extensive display of grotesques. First to appear are those on the St. Swithun's building which faces the High just past the corner of Longwall Street. Here is the Green Man with the headress of grapes and vine leaves (p. 17, 5). Further on is the piper (p.3,3); perhaps the carver enjoyed having a dig at another artistic profession. Next we come to a gateway arch, now seldom used. On its sloping side squats a most likeable and indomitable dragon, puffing away on its Churchillian rainwater cigar (p. 27, 5). Its companion on the other side of the arch is giving a smart, left-handed salute.

You should look at the carvings on the rest of the High Street front and on the Tower before entering the college, and from the other side of the road. You will already have seen some of them in the introduction. Those on the front were carved by the Cheltenham based carver Pat Conoley (p. 7,3 p.2, 1 & 2). Magdalen Tower has just undergone the most thorough restoration of its entire history and shines pristine in Clipsham and various French limestones, Savonnières-Courteraie, Anstrude Jaune and Massangis. Its carvings, too, have been completely replaced, since the old ones had decayed beyond saving. Oxford's prevailing south-west winds used to bring the sulphurous fumes from the Gas Works beyond Folly Bridge across to Christ Church, Merton and Magdalen and the higher carvings suffered accordingly. The work was shared between Pat Conoley, Percy Quick and Michael Groser, and was done between 1977 and 1981. Pat Conoley was responsible for the designs, which were based as far as possible on the previous figures. Some no longer had any recognisable shape and it was decided to replace these by heads of senior and long-serving members of the College, both fellows and staff. There are two lines of carvings around the top of the Tower. In the lower line are the dons and staff, all respectful likenesses. However, if you look along the upper line, you will find something rather different. Here the caricaturists have been at work, selecting their targets from their own working company. On the far, eastern side of the tower is Mr. Myles, managing director of Axtell, Perry and Symm, represented as a human headed lion (6). Clearly visible on the south-east corner is Mr Biscoe-Taylor, surveyor-in-charge of the restoration, looking remarkably like a certain member of the Royal Family (1). On the south-west are Mr. Upstone, draughtsman, in glasses, and Mr Cooper, assistant to the surveyor-in-charge, the length of whose nose time will doubtless diminish. There is Mr. Hale, site foreman, angelic and frizzled, and last to view a winged Mr. Quick (3). He carved his boss's caricature; the other heads shown here were carved by Michael Groser. Whether or not their various facial peculiarities have been accurately represented, you may judge from the evidence here assembled (2, 4, 5, 7).

It is now time to consider exactly how these figures are made and put in place. If you have a picture of a carver clinging precariously to the side of the Tower tapping at a lump of stone, you should discard it. The work is almost invariably done at ground level, in yard or studio. Each figure is carved as part of its supporting block, so that when in place the greater part of the whole remains hidden. The block is first roughed out, perhaps using power assisted tools of some kind, then more and more detail is put in by hand. The chisel's abrasive action, often producing sparks, creates a protective surface on the stone which allows it to weather out its first few years before the regular hardening builds up. The blocks must be carefully matched to their future resting places. A figure intended for the corner immediately next to Magdalen's front entrance will lie for ever in one of the college outbuildings; it was carved on a right-angled block but, as you can see, the corner happened to be a ninety-five degree one. The figures generally weigh several

hundred pounds. Those on the side of Merton chapel, with their own length of stone behind them, weighed a ton and went in by crane. Those for Magdalen Tower went up on a specially installed platform lift. Less distant hoists are made by mechanical line and pulley. The carvings are always treated with the utmost care, as a careless knock could lose them a wing or an ear.

Picture (3) shows a number of grotesques waiting to be taken to the very top of Magdalen Tower. You can see how the supporting blocks have been carefully angled to fit the pinnacles. Pictures (1) and (2) show the completion of the whole process; an eagle is fitted to its final resting place by Mr. Gary Hale, with the assistance of Mr. Eddie Collins and the arm and shoulder of Mr. Kevin Dean. Gary is the son of Mick Hale (p. 19, 3 & 5); his grandfather and great-grandfather, too, were master masons.

As you enter Magdalen, you see some of Percy Quick's best grotesques to your right on the west end of the chapel (4–6). One might expect the carver of such ebullient figures to be a hearty, vigorous extravert. Mr. Quick is, however, quite the opposite; sensitive and quiet, even shy, he gives the impression of a certain frailty. He take a business-like attitude to his work. He enjoys carving grotesques; one reason is that "if you knock a finger off, no one notices." (Carvers never know precisely the quality of the stone beneath their chisels and such things can occasionally happen even to the most experienced).

Through the arch on the right of the chapel is a triangular quad. The figures there are the work of Mr. Thomas Tyrrell, who was for many years a mason on the college staff. He was a natural carver, and when there was time to spare from other work he would cut a grotesque ready for use when required. Notice his various demons, especially the ones immediately above the quad's narrow entrance. The entrance to the chapel is on its north side and is reached by returning through the front quad. On the roof of its porch are plaster bosses, including Magdalen's oldest Green Man, put up by James Wyatt during his restoration of 1790. There is also a Green Man boss on the roof of the west end of the chapel. Look also for the frieze of musician angels along the organ screen — quaint rather than grotesque — and let their gentle sweetness prepare you for what is to come.

1 & 2 An eagle is placed in its nest in Christ Church cloisters.

3 A grotto of grotesques awaits elevation.

4, 5, 6 & 7 Above are three of the grotesques on the west end of Magdalen chapel. The party beneath have just arrived in St. John's Quad and are looking up at them. Above, the boys pulling the grotesque mouth are enjoying themselves; the boy on the right, squashed under an extraneous limb, looks apprehensive. Their various expressions of pleasure and bemusement seem mirrored on the youthful faces below. (Another carving, further to the left, has a monster crunching a child in its jaws). It is clearly winter, which shows that you can go gargoyle viewing at any time of the year.

4

5

6

7

1

Three of Magdalen College's most remarkable carvings.

1 Man-monster and alligator are locked in symbiotic conflict, each grasping the other's tongue.

2 Once more the grasping of the tongue. This seems not so much an escape as a benign monster being attended to by his valet.

3 Kings fighting with swords, or pastry cooks with pallet knives? Ecclesiastics, perhaps, presenting points of dogma.

For in the cloisters beyond are the most extraordinary carvings of the tour. Set on pedestals around three of its four sides are twenty two statues, human, biblical and monstrous. Let their total impression sweep over you before you view them individually or try to interpret them. Generations of students have wondered at them from their windows; for nearly five hundred years plays have been performed and parties held before their watchful eyes. They were installed in 1508–9, not long after the founding of the college. In 1605 they were painted (or repainted rather, for it was then the practice to colour carved stonework) in honour of a visit by Prince Henry, the eldest son of King James I. The horned figure in the north west corner, it is recorded, was decked out in sky blue.

They well deserve their name of the "heiroglyphicals"; an interpretation of them would provide material for several Ph.D.'s. They must surely have a meaning; allegorical figures were popular in the sixteenth century, and the college went to considerable trouble and expense to erect them. The original key was, however, soon lost. In 1727 the well-known antiquarian William Stukely described them as "whimsical figures" which "amuse the vulgar" but are nothing more than "the licentious inventions of the mason." He had not done his homework, for in the 1670's Dr. Henry Clerk, the President of the college, specially requested one of his Fellows, Dr. William Reeks, to provide an interpretation of them. This Reeks did, in the form of a sixty page Latin manuscript treatise entitled *Oedipus Magdaleniensis*. The title does not make him a forerunner of Freud; he simply meant that he was confronting riddles as puzzling as that of the Sphinx. He decided that they represented various virtues and vices connected with the academic life. A summary of his findings appeared in John Carter's *Specimens of the Ancient Painting and Sculpture in England* (1887). You can follow his conclusions around the circle.

"Beginning therefore from the south-west corner, the two first figures we meet with are the Lion and the Pelican. The former of these is an emblem of Courage and Vigilance, the latter of parental Affection and Tenderness. Both of them express to us the complete character of a good governor of a college. Accordingly they are placed under the windows of those lodgings which originally belonged to the president, as the instructions they convey ought particularly to regulate his conduct. Going on to the right hand side, on the other side of the gateway, are four figures viz. the Schoolmaster, the Physician, the Lawyer and the Divine. These are ranged along the outside of the library, and represent the duties and business of the students of the house. By means of learning in general, they are to be introduced to one of these learned professions, or else, as is hinted to us by the figure with the cap and bells in the corner, they must turn out fools in the end.

We now come to the north side of the quadrangle, and here the first three figures represent the history of David, his conquest over the Lion and Goliath; from whence we are taught not to be discouraged by any difficulties that may stand in our way, as the vigour of youth will easily enable us to surmount them. The next figure to these is that of the hippopotamus or river-horse, carrying his young ones upon his shoulder. This is an emblem of a good tutor, or fellow of the college, who is set to watch over the youth of society and by whose prudence they are to be led through the dangers of their first entry into the world. The figure immediately following represents Sobriety or Temperance, that most necessary virtue of a collegiate life. The whole remaining train of figures are the vices we are instructed to avoid. Those next to Temperance are the opposite vices of Gluttony and Drunkeness. Then follow the Lucanthropus, the Hyena and Panther representing Violence, Fraud and Treachery: the Griffin representing Covetousness, and the next figure Anger or moroseness: the Dog, the Dragon and the Deer, Flattery, Envy and Timidity: and the three last the Mantichora, the Boxers and the Lamia, Pride, Contention and Lust."

These strange and monstrous figures are representative of the twenty two "heiroglyphicals" which stand in Magdalen College cloisters.

1 Gluttony seems to most likely interpretation of this face-in-belly figure, which stands at the end of the line of monstrous vices.

2 According to William Reeks, seventeenth century fellow of the college, we have here a lawyer consulting his client, the law being one of the professions suitable for graduates to enter. They are, however, in very close consultation and others have seen them as Jacob wrestling with the Angel, so linking them with the Biblical figures which occupy the next five places in the circle. This photograph was taken in 1872, when the figure on the right was completely swathed in ivy, making him more like a Green Man.

3 Wysteria now laps but does not yet conceal the virtuous hippopotamus, which carries its young one upon its back as a tutor should care for his students.

4 Fraud is not all he seems to be. He presents a human head, but his true nature is dinosaurian.

3

4

Reeks' basic scheme seems the most likely one. Some of his interpretations are those of the old bestiaries. The lion sleeps with his eyes open and is therefore a symbol of watchfulness. The pelican wounds its own breast in order to resurrect its young (which it has previously slain) with its blood. Other interpretations seem more open. Reeks' lawyer is supposed to be advising a client, but others have seen him as Jacob wrestling with the Angel (p. 25, 2). His "divine" is Moses carrying the Tables of the Law. Moses was often represented as horned, by Michaelangelo among others, and this came about because of a mistranslation. As he came down from Mount Sinai his face "shone", but the Latin Vulgate translated the Hebrew for shining as "cornatu", meaning horned; the roots of the two Hebrew words are very similar. Moses' companion in the north-west corner may not therefore be a fool with bells, but Aaron; in Deuteronomy, Aaron's robe was decorated with pomegranites and balls of gold, and he is so represented in some mediaeval carving. One would not expect to see Aaron with lion's paws, but photographic records show that these were added in 1867 when many of the figures along the north side were recarved. Perhaps he once had a noble face, but the carver of 1867 reproduced what time and the weather had made of him. It was then that the subduer of the lion (David, or perhaps Samson) acquired his very clerkly features. One suspects a contemporary caricature, for the previous figure is quite different; the present one looks more like a don sniffing out a syllogism than a hero wresting sweetness from the jaws of death.

The most striking of the statues are, of course, the monsters. Some seem completely saurian, a product of that primitive level of evolutionary consciousness when Life's highest expression was the dinosaur. One cannot be sure exactly what they represent. The griffin was said to guard hidden treasure in the deserts of India and is an apt symbol of covetousness. "Fraud" (p. 25, 4) holds an owl, a creature of darkness, and a detached, deceptive head; (by 1867 its own head was unrecognisable as a hyena or anything else and it was given the one it has today). But what is one to make of this composite creature (3), two-headed, breasted (fraud's spouse perhaps) and its attendant rabbit? The dog, a neat grey hound, has a stone collar; the monster second on its right has for some reason an iron coronet as a collar, and is fastened to the wall by a chain.

The nineteenth century saw the wholesale renewal of the grotesques on

3

1

2

4

5

4 Magdalen has many demons, keeping watch from wall and tower. Here is a typical one of their number, with cloak of shadow.

5 This Churchillian dragon welcomed you to Magdalen College and now speeds you on your way.

1 No putti these. Lichen has given her a leopard-skin stole, but little else.

2 A piece of erotic play carved, surprisingly enough, around 1880.

3 This monster beggars interpretation. Its complexity might even suggest an alchemical origin.

the walls of the cloisters. At their best, the Victorian carvers of Magdalen showed surreal powers of imagination and considerable technical skill. Some of the most interesting figures are on the outside east wall (centrefold, 1–3); you reach these by going round the cloisters and through the arch on that side. An erotic element was common in mediaeval carving, even on churches: in Oxford it appears very occasionally. This girl tucked away in the north east corner of the cloisters has a certain wayward charm (1), and there can be no doubt about the wickedness of this pair (2), who are in one of the private parts of the College. Of course modern taste would not find them offensive, but one is surprised that no Victorian divine took an outraged chisel to the carving.

Mention of divines and chisels brings one to the Rev. Dr. Ellerton. He was elected a Fellow in 1805 and was for many years college bursar and librarian. He deserves a place in the guide, if only for having saved the cloisters from destruction. One late summer he returned from his vacation to find that certain architects and builders, in premature pursuit of one of Magdalen's many proposed schemes of alteration, had demolished the whole of their north side; as bursar he put a stop to this and had the range rebuilt as it was before. Ellerton was a considerable eccentric; he was rector of the village of Horspath and once took up a special collection among his colleagues for a poor family who were being hounded by an oppressive landlord; later it was discovered that the landlord was Ellerton himself. He was fiercely anti-papal in his religious views and critical of church ritual. It is said that a Catholic carver made a likeness of him wearing a mitre, and in fact the figures on both the corners of the outside, north wall of the cloisters are mitred. The other story is that certain undergraduates bribed a carver to put up a caricature of him. When Ellerton saw it, he was so angry that he ordered it to be defaced. Ever afterwards, he was obliged to look across from his library at its broken nose and scored brows and, as the years progressed, he found that he was growing more and more to resemble it. The figure he would have seen is the one on the far, north-east corner. It is, however, youthful and smooth of face. Either Ellerton's passage to eternity worked another transformation on it or, as is more likely, the damaged figure was later replaced by another designed to match the one on the opposite corner. (The story has an immediately striking affinity to that of Oscar Wilde's *The Picture of Dorian Grey* and it is worth recalling that Wilde spent four years as a student at Magdalen).

In Magdalen almost every wall and tower is encrusted with demons. They seem such an integral part of their surroundings that it is time to address the question again: why are they there? Christianity sets good and evil firmly apart; it is possible that demons were originally put on Christian buildings to remind people of hell and of damnation. In this secular and psychological age we would be more inclined to give the demons our sympathy, seeing them as aspects of our own horny, scaly selves. Yet the conflict between good and evil is not over. Surely F. Bligh Bond, architect, architectural historian and uncoverer of the mysteries of Glastonbury, was nearer the truth when he said that in its grotesques "the Church overcomes and converts to good uses even the most monstrous forms of evil." My own feelings on the matter are these: Man's sacred towers aspire to clarity and light. The murky forces of confusion which swirl about them are unsubtle, unintelligent; to be dispelled, they must be met by countenances like their own which they will understand, fierce, even contorted, though backed by the will to order and to light. Exalted angels like St. Michael work against spiritual wickedness in high places; they need their lowlier minions who cope with this kind of quotidian chaos. These ever-present demons are therefore like little psychic vacuum cleaners, sucking up and voiding forth the dust and silt, the lollocks and the lesser ghouls, the fears and frustrations, which accumulate around our days.

28

St. Edmund Hall

These thoughts came to me not at my desk but as an inspiration as I was clambering over the battlements and roof of the ancient church of St. Peter-in-the-East. St. Peter's is now the library of St. Edmund Hall and it is there that the tour now proceeds, up the High Street and right into Queen's Lane. (You may, if you like, make a short detour up the High to see the towers of University College, which have some fine grotesques by Percy Quick). You reach the former church by going into the college and through the arch to the left. The churchyard, with its ancient walls and ivy covered tombs, is a marvellously peaceful place. Some of the carvings seem of considerable age. Some have been replaced, some have not. Over the porch are several vacant places; one can imagine their gargoyles flying off one All Souls' Night to trysts from which they never returned.

Around the top of the tower have been placed the heads of people connected with the church's restoration and conversion in the late 1960's, five of them being fellows of the college. Michael Groser was the carver and

he has highlighted his subjects' special features. Over the porch is the Rev. Dr. J. N. D. Kelly, formerly Principal of the college (1). Next to him is Mr. R. E. Alton; he was bursar at the time of the restoration and therefore holds two money bags (3). In the middle of the eastern side of the tower is the Rev. Graham Midgley, dog-collared, with his dog Fred, similarly attired (5). Mr. Midgley, formerly Dean and Chaplain of the college, has lived all his academic life companioned by one or more yellow labradors. Close by him is the legal head of Mr. Jeffrey Hackney (7). All these gentlemen kindly allowed their living selves to be matched with their stone counterparts (2,4,6,8). They cannot be said, like Dr. Ellerton, to have grown more and more like their gargoyles; nevertheless, after seventeen years the likenesses are still remarkably good. Fred sent his living representative, William, to be photographed. His passing occasioned the following epitaph from his owner, as a fine a piece of dog-gerel verse as one could wish to see.

Beneath this turf the Dean's dog Fred
Without his master, goes to Earth, stone dead.
But on the tower, stone Dean and Fred together
Enjoy the sunshine and endure bad weather.

The fifth and last Fellow is the late Dr. Emden, who is on the south-east corner. He presented Michael Groser with the problem of how to carve spectacles in stone. And what of the master himself? He too is on the tower, in the middle of the east, road side (overleaf, 1) — appropriately, since you are about to see, at New College, the greatest range of his work.

7

8

1&2 Rev. Dr Kelly was Principal of the college. He used to play squash regularly up to the time of his retirement and remained a good match for his undergraduate opponents.

3&4 Mr. Alton was college bursar at the time of the restoration, hence the money bags. He says that his carving bears a strong resemblance to the figure of Avarice at Autun in France, though he does not consider avarice, however appropriate for a bursar, to be one of his besetting sins.

5&6 Rev. Graham Midgley was Dean and Chaplain of St. Edmund Hall and has lived all his academic life companioned by one or more yellow labradors. He is looking up at his likeness on the tower, but William seems more interested in the camera.

7&8 Mr. Hackney's carving is bewigged and banded in recognition of the terms he spent on leave practising at the Chancery Bar. He was college librarian and had a room high up in the tower, like an owl in the former belfry.

1

2

1 Michael Groser's self portrait is on the east, road side of the St. Edmund Hall library tower.

2 Here he is thoughtfully roughing out a block destined to become a panel for the House of Commons. Carving is a dusty business, hence the daily newspaper hat.

3 Perhaps the most striking of the New College Lane heads, on the extreme left of the line. Placed in close juxtaposition to its creator, does it not resemble his own demonic mask?

4 Two squirrels gather nuts from the wall overlooking New College Lane.

5 A South American lemur prepares to leap from the same wall.

6 This crested fish swims among the animal-humans on the side of New College Chapel.

7 An afterword; an uninentional self portrait situated on the roof of the Chapel for the benefit of passing birds and angels.

3

7

New College

4

5

6

Michael Groser (2) has lived and worked in Oxford since 1955. He trained first at Leeds College of Art while working as a miner during the war, and afterwards at St. Martin's College of Art in London. He has always combined carving and music; he sang at Westminster Abbey and St. Paul's Cathedral and was for many years a member of the choir at New College. Friendly, self effacing, he has something of the simplicity of the saint and the absent mindedness of a professor. His practice is to work freely from his imagination. The first designs he made for New College were based on models from the past, but Mr Geoffrey Beard, architect to the college, pronounced them "constipated" and encouraged him to use his own inventiveness. It was good advice.

His carvings at New College fall into three groups. The first is in some ways the best known because it is the most clearly visible; you see it from the middle section of the Lane on the southernmost wall of the college. Half of the carvings are heads (3; p35, 1; p43,2). They are subtly designed; you can play with their shapes, turning them into geometric forms and back again into heads. The other half of the group are animals of all kinds, from a lively South American lemur (5) to scarab beetles on a lump of dung.

The second group is inside the college, along the chapel on the north side of the Front Quad. Many of these are animals, not real this time but fantastical and anthropomorphised (6). People say they look like an aunt or an old tutor, but no reference to anyone living or dead is intended. Others say they are the animals they see in their dreams.

The third group is approached from the cloisters. Around the Bell Tower which rises above them is a remarkable series of heads. Some of them are well known; what fewer people know is that they have a carefully planned symbolism. Those on the south side of the tower, visible from the cloisters, represent the seven virtues of patience, generosity, charity, prayerfulness, innocent love, enthusiastic joy and justice. Those on the opposite, north side symbolise the exactly corresponding vices; these are the Seven Deadly Sins of anger, gluttony, envy, pride, lust, accidie (sloth) and avarice. The virtues are visible to all; however, the vices can only be seen from a part of the college not open to the public. New College values its academic calm and you should respect it; moreover, the vices are clearly revealed in our photographs (p. 34–35). One could spend pages describing these heads — unnecessarily, for they themselves do it all. Only one obvious point needs to be made: the importance of the hands. Michael Groser had the idea of including hands only after he had carved the first head; they certainly add greatly to their expressiveness. Patience endures her hands chained. Generosity is dividing a piece of bread, while gluttony stuffs a slab of it into his fat mouth. Lust (to be understood as corrupt as opposed to innocent love) is holding a pornographic book. The hands of avarice are tightly clenched while justice, weighing both sides, has one hand open and one hand closed. (This you can see only by standing in the little alley immediately below the west end of the chapel. From here you can also catch a sideways glimpse of the heads on the east side of the tower; they are self-righteousness, Eve, despair and the terror of death).

The cloisters have become the refuge of the saints taken down from St. Mary's tower at the time of Jackson's restoration. As you leave them you should go into the chapel and see Epstein's famous statue of Lazarus rising from the dead, which is at the west end. Head twisted unnaturally back, he struggles to escape the grave cloths twisted around him. Many people have disliked the statue; the Russian leader Nikita Krushchev complained that it had given him a sleepless night. All that you have seen on this tour may help you to appreciate it more fully, for it is precisely the grotesque element, so often used by artists of the twentieth century, that gives it much of its power.

32

1

2

THE SEVEN VIRTUES

Looking down on New College cloisters are these beautiful and expressive heads, representing seven virtues. Being on the south side of the Bell Tower, they are touched by the sun of grace and illumination. From left to right, they are:

1. Patience
2. Generosity
3. Charity
4. Prayerfulness
5. Innocent love
6. Enthusiastic joy
7. Justice

3

4

7

5

6

THE SEVEN VICES

On the cold north side of New College
Bell Tower, where the sun hardly
reaches, are the Seven Deadly Sins:
1. Anger
2. Gluttony
3. Envy
4. Pride
5. Corrupt love
6. Accidie (sloth)
7. Avarice

The New College Bell Tower gets a
reminder of its function from these
topmost figures carved around its
turret.

1 These well known heads are neither emperors nor philosophers. At night they are said to come down from their pedestals and go drinking in local pubs, but that cannot be vouched for either. They have been twice replaced during their history. What is their true background and identity?

2 An answer from the past: one of the original set of heads carved during the 1660's and still surviving.

The Sheldonian Herms

Emerging from New College, we pass again between high, blackened walls; it is difficult to realise that twenty-five years ago the greater part of Oxford's stonework was in a comparable state. These walls are made of great blocks of hardstone quarried at Headington in the fourteenth century; the toolmarks on them are still visible. The writer and humourist Max Beerbohm called this "the dark ravine which leads to New College" and Beerbohm should be in your minds as your journey returns to its starting point and you re-approach the heads around the Sheldonian Theatre. It was he who first called them Emperors, in his famous novel *Zuleika Dobson* published in 1911. Zuleika, the beautiful and much feted conjuress and granddaughter of the Warden of Judas College, pays a week-end visit to Oxford. Everyone, including the supremely gifted young dandy the Duke of Dorset, falls in love with her. However, Zuleika can love no one who loves her, and the entire student body ends by comitting suicide in the Thames after the May races. The Sheldonian heads act as a prophetic chorus to the tragedy; on the first evening of Zuleika's visit an old don, emerging from Blackwell's, sees great beads of perspiration glistening on their brows. By calling them Roman Emperors, Beerbohm gives himself the opportunity for some fine rhetoric.

. . ."Here in Oxford, exposed eternally and inexorably to wind and frost, to the four winds that lash them and the rains that wear them away, they are expiating, in effigy, the abominations of their pride and cruelty and lust. Who were lechers, they are without bodies; who were tyrants, they are crowned never but with crowns of snow; who made themselves even with the gods, they are by American visitors frequently mistaken for the Twelve Apostles". . .

Poor heads! Others know them as philosophers, though they look even less philosophical than imperial. What is their real identity?

The original heads were set up at the time of the building of the Sheldonian in 1662–9 (2). The Theatre was the first work of the young and brilliant Christopher Wren, then Professor of Mathematics and Astronomy. Perhaps Wren got the idea for them from some classical, double-headed Janus figures which he had recently seen at a chateaux at Vaux le Vicomte, near Paris; he was certainly following the Oxford tradition of architectural carving. The heads were commissioned from the master mason William Byrd, who had a yard nearby on the present site of Hertford College. Wren and Byrd were friends; it appears that they had worked together on a method of staining marble a deep red. The original building accounts describe Byrd's heads as "termains", which links them with the Roman god Terminus who presided over boundaries and boundary stones. The Greeks would have called them Herms, after Hermes as god of doorways. Such heads were placed at the entrances to temples and private houses; the mutilation of the Herms of Athens in 415 B.C., an act of gross impiety intended to incriminate Alcibiades, is a well known event in classical history. These, then, are the Sheldonian Herms; high up on their railings, they do indeed provide an impressive guard for what was the University's first own secular assembly hall.

In 1868, a new set of heads was installed. Oral tradition has it that the faces were modelled on those of the workmen in the yard in George Street where they were carved. Soon after they were put up, undergraduates daubed them with paint; the removal of the paint started them decaying rapidly. Many in Oxford remember them as they were in the 1960's: blank, pitted and almost featureless. Replacement was proposed; one dissenter was the sculptor Henry Moore, who admired their time-worn quality. However, the project went ahead and between 1970 and 1972 Mr. Michael Black carved thirteen new heads. His commission was to get as near as possible to the originals,

2 This engraving is from David Loggan's *Oxonia Illustrata* published in 1675 very shortly after the completion of the Sheldonian. It effectively shows the fortress-like character of the University's first own assembly hall, before it was surrounded by other buildings. Riots between town and gown were still common in those days, so protection was needed. Woe betide the townsman who tried to climb these railings and pass these staring guardians.

and if you look carefully at the detail of the Loggan engraving, which he used (the Bodleian Library photographers provided him with special enlargements of each of the heads) you can see how close he has come. He also studied the original heads themselves which it turned out, had survived in various North Oxford gardens; there are two in the Provost's garden at Worcester College. (It was intended to preserve the second set of heads for posterity; they were removed most carefully, but when the lorry carrying them braked rather sharply at the first set of traffic lights, they fell completely to pieces). Mr. Black was helped in the carving by two assistants. The first head took him three hundred hours, the last thirty. Later, he completed the line by carving four more heads for the Museum of Science.

The heads are crowned not with vine or laurel but with ivy, which remains green throughout the winter. (There may be another Janus connection here, for Janus was the god both of doorways and of the New Year). There is an ivy bush in a corner of the Botanical Gardens which was growing when William Byrd carved the first heads; perhaps he took it as his model. You will see their crowns most clearly if you approach them from behind, from between the Bodleian Library and the Clarendon building. Notice that one of them has a "bird" nestling in the ivy.

Their reputation as Emperors helped Michael Black when he was discussing the head of Sir Alec Douglas-Hume which he recently carved for

1

1 The new Herms have just been completed and are about to make the journey up from their birthplace in a Binsey meadow. Their carver has got so caught up in his creations that he has become one of them.

the House of Lords with one of Sir Alec's successors. "Were you not," she asked, "overawed at having to carve a former Prime Minister?" Now Michael Black is not a man to be overawed by anyone; he lives by creative energy, humour (1) and an unconcern for authority. However, he was able to turn the question in a gentlmanly way: "After spending so long with so many Roman Emperors — no."

The thirteen heads may, according to their carver, be seen as a history of beards. They move outwards from the centre in matching pairs. The beards of the heads each side of the central gateway are rough and unkempt, while the beard of the seventh head is a carded and combed creation worthy of Charles II himself. I have presumed to give each of them a name and to arrange them in the form of the fantasy on the opposite page. It might be called Byrd and Black's Bevy of Beards. The seven are:

1. The beard barbaric

7. The beard beaumonde

2. The beard bacchic

6. The beard beaver

4. The beard bosky

3. The beard bifurcated

5. The beard bobbed

1   2

In Eden Garden

Now that you have completed the main part of the tour, various further
possibilities present themselves. If it is still early and you wish to relax
among greenery, you may pay a visit to **Exeter College** and its beautiful
Fellows Garden, which is open to the public from 2 to 4 pm. From it you
look up at the carvings on the south side of the Duke Humphrey Library.
The doorway which gives access to the garden is on the east side of the front
quad opposite the main gateway. Here you can keep company with John
Sparrow, former Warden of All Souls, flanked by bird and unicorn (he is on
the corner of the Selden End, looking towards his old college) and be
serenaded by a mermaid with golden hair and looking glass.

If the time is late and you would like liquid refreshment, you should
return along New College Lane and take an immediate turn left down St.
Helen's Passage to the **Turf Tavern**, one of Oxford's two oldest pubs. It
used to be known as a centre for gaming and betting, and the way to it was
called Hell Passage. From either of its gardens you get a uniquely good view
of the west side of New College Bell Tower. On the left hand corner is a
grasping avarice and past him you get a slanting view of New College's
hidden vices. Facing you are various figures, including the Tempter (2) and
the Tempted (1). Should you see them as accusers; should you let them put
you off your pint? Surely not. In the humour of their carving there is the
wisdom of experience. They have understood the human conscience; they
have gone beyond fanaticism. Guilt once understood becomes powerless, a
butt for humour, even. That, too, is one of the lessons which the grotesques
have to teach. One the other side of the tower is sweet Eve, holding the
apple by which man gained knowledge of good and evil, the head next to
her convulsed in a parody of self-righteous disapproval (3).

1 & 2 From his corner of the New
College Bell Tower the beckoning
tempter (2) demonstrates his power. He
seems to have deceitfully convinced his
victim (1) that his surrender and its
unpleasant consequences are inevitable.

4 & 5 On the Wadham College
gateway tower is Nicholas Wadham, its
founder, portrayed as a rose, and his
wife Dorothy, surmounted by a scallop
shell.

6 On the dome of Rhodes House is this
bird from the ancient, ruined city of
Zimbabwe.

3 On the opposite side of the tower,
Eve prepares to eat the apple. The
gargoyle next to her is a horrified
witness of Man's fall, but without it
there would have been no Incarnation
and no Redemption. It is as the carol
says,

*'Ne had the apple taken been, the
        apple taken been,
Ne had never Our Lady a been
        Heavené Queen.
Blesséd be the time that apple taken was.
Therefore we maun singen Deo Gracias.'*

3

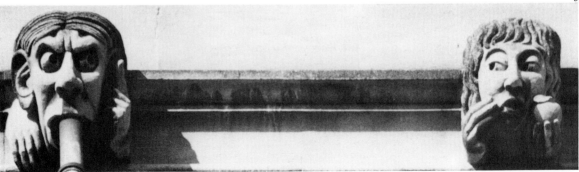

4

5

6

The Minute Particulars of Mankind

If you are getting a stiff neck from looking up so much, you might like to go along Broad Street to **Balliol College**, where the figures are close to the ground. The library, on the left of the front quad, has some amusing eye level representations of scholarship and devotion and their attendant distractions of drunkeness and gluttony. Among the heads of various anonymous donors along the old library facing the entrance, Michael Groser has placed his father; he was a well known priest in the East End of London, and appears here as a mitred bishop.

If you are interested in Max Beerbohm and his Emperors, you might like to continue along Broad Street and turn right to the **Randolph Hotel**, where there is a fine series of cartoons by Osbert Lancaster based on his book Zuleika Dobson; the one showing the beads of perspiration on the Emperor's brows is in the dining room. The Randolph, built in 1868, has its own tiny sets of grotesques under the two large bay windows at the front. In place of one of the little, hissing dragons, the carver has put a portrait of a pet spaniel. How often must this kind of thing been done! In the Schools Quadrangle of the Bodleian, above the door to the Schola Metaphysicae, is a carving of Jess, a Shetland sheepdog which belonged to Miss Margaret Crum, who worked for many years in the music section of the Library.

From the Randolph it is a short step across to **St. John's College**, whose Canterbury Quad with its remarkable drainheads has already been twice mentioned.

Family portraits are also in evidence on the gateway tower of **Wadham College**, which is at the bottom of South Parks Road. There is Nicholas Wadham, the founder of the college, represented as a rose — a floreate head, one might say (4). The rose was part of his family coat of arms. There too is his wife Dorothy, shaded by the scallop shell from the Petre family arms (5). Between them, also carved by Michael Black, is a modern foliate head, in which foliage and head have merged.

Towards a Universal View

The apotheosis of your journey takes you from Broad Street up South Parks Road. Oxford has had, through learning and through empire, links with almost every part of the world, and you will see just how universal is the carved beast and the protective, grimacing face. From Broad Street, you can see Exeter College chapel rising above the buildings. It was closely modelled on the Church of Sainte Chappelle in Paris; around its dark and narrow spire are set eight demon princelings of the air. On the corner of Catte St. and Holywell is the old **Indian Institute**, inaugurated amidst much splendour by the Prince of Wales in 1883. In decorating the corner tower, Mr. Aumonier of Symm and Co. adapted his Palladian manner to Indian forms. The most interesting of these is an elephant; partial cleaning has made it look as if emerging from a bath in a muddy river. There is also a handsome golden elephant on the weathervane of the building.

On the corner of South Parks Road and Parks Road stands **Rhodes House**, dedicated to Commonwealth studies. Upon its rounded, green copper dome stands what appears at first sight to be a griffin. It is in fact an African bird, a copy of one of the soapstone carvings found in the ruins of the ancient city of Zimbabwe. The early Shona people built the city during our mediaeval period and the bird is thought to be the oracular fish-eagle, bringer of rain and lightning and symbol of fertility (6).

On the other side of South Parks Road, is the Victorian Gothic of **Keble College**. The Warden's Lodgings on the corner is guarded, like the palace of some Eastern potentate, by flying dragons (some headless). Opposite, set back from the road, are the **University** and **Pitt Rivers Museums**.

42

1 In 1859, a photograph was taken of one of the O'Shea brothers carving his controversial monkeys and cats on one of the windows of the University Museum. This portion of it shows O'Shea at work; the cats and monkeys can still be seen today.

Acknowledgements

We would like to thank all those who have helped in the compilation of this book: those carvers, masons and architects, scholars, archivists and librarians, and college and ecclesiastical authorities without whom it could not have come into existence. We would also like to thank Ralph Coward for the map, Robert Valentine for the artwork of the Bevy of Beards, Jerry Burman for his work on the design and George Matthews for photographic assistance.

Acknowledgements are also due on the following photographs:

p. 20,3. A. L. Mount, Clerk of Works, Magdalen College.
p. 21,7. Martin Stott.
p. 24–5,2. New College Archives, reproduction by Bodleian Library.
p. 30,7. Geoffrey Beard.
p. 36,2. Guido Ditella.
p. 37,2. Bodleian Library, from Arch. Antiq. II. 13.
p. 38,1. Oxford Mail & Times.
p. 43,3. Pitts Rivers Museum.

Charon Press, 104 Ferry Road, Oxford OX3 0EX.

Together they offer us a wealth of natural and cultural forms. The University Museum is an altogether remarkable building. John Ruskin was its chief inspirer; he conceived it as a Gothic temple of Knowledge, and its decorations were intended to represent the physical cosmos in all its aspects. A Dublin firm of architects, Deane and Woodward, were engaged to erect the building. They brought with them several carvers, the most notable of whom were the brothers O'Shea, who set to work inscribing the fauna of the planet around the windows at the front of the building. However, all did not run smoothly. The O'Sheas' free-ranging style — Dr. Acland, the Professor of Medicine and the other chief instigator of the project, called it "gurgoyle-like" — did not appeal to all tastes. Acland tells the following story.

"O'Shea rushed into my home one afternoon and — in a state of wild excitement — related as follows: "The Master of the University (that is, Dr. Plumtre, Master of University College and secretary of the University committee supervising the building) found me on my scaffold just now. "What are you doing?" says he. "Monkeys," said I. "Come down directly," says he, "you shall not destroy the property of the University.""" Acland was unable to resolve the situation, and the following day O'Shea was back at the window carving cats. This time he succeeded in frightening Dr. Plumtre away with his protestations. The window in question, complete with cats and monkeys, can be seen to the right of the main entrance, and there is also a contemporary photograph of O'Shea at work on it (1).

The respite did not last long, however, and shortly afterwards O'Shea was dismissed. Acland found him in the porch, "wielding heavy blows such as one imagines Michael Angelo might have struck when he was first blocking out the design of some immortal work. "What are you doing?" I asked. "I thought you were gone, and Mr. Woodward has given no design for the long moulding in the hard green stone." Striking on still, O'Shea shouted, "Parrhots and Owwls! Parrhots and Owwls! Members of Convocation!" There they were, blocked out alternately." Acland ordered the dons' heads removed. If you look carefully at the porch, you will find the parrots and the owls on the upper mouldings, but the two outside columns of hard, green stone are noticeably absent. The following year however, the brothers were back at work. Each day they would receive new specimens from the Botanical Gardens and carve vivid likenesses of them on the bases of the pillars around the lower gallery.

There are many other things in the Museum of relevant interest. The rearing dinosaur is surely the natural prototype of some of the monsters you have just seen. At the rear of the upper gallery is an exhibition of the different kinds of stone which have been used in the building of Oxford. Then, if it is between two and four o'clock in the afternoon, you should go through to the Pitt Rivers Museum. As you enter the lower gallery, you see cases containing masks from many different parts of the world. It becomes clear that the magical and ritual use of grotesque carving is as broad as the human race. There are leering, red masks used by Korean Buddhist monks to exorcise evil spirits, and masks with huge ears and noses used by the shamans of Central Borneo to enter the afterworld and bring back the souls of the sick. There are the intricate and terrifying masks used by Tibetans in ritual dances to ward off evil and misfortune; so fierce are these that the early missionaries thought that the Tibetans were devil-worshippers. There are the more purely theatrical demon masks used in the Japanese Noh theatre. In the case opposite there are masks from the South Seas of amazingly beautiful and original design; anyone planning to carve a gargoyle would do well to study them. Lastly, at the back of the gallary there rises what is undoubtedly Oxford's largest grotesque, a forty foot high Indian totem pole from Queen Charlotte Island off the Pacific coast of British Columbia. It stood outside the chief's house and ensured his well-being and prosperity. You also, who have traced a magic circle through the city of Oxford and kept company with her protectors, will no doubt have earned good fortune for yourselves.

As imagination sinks into stillness, so the stones which it has shaped become charged with powers of movement. The traditions and stories to this effect are many. At night the guardians of the Sheldonian get down from their pedestals and slake their thirsts in local pubs; one can imagine them propped on stools around the bar of the King's Arms opposite exchanging epigrams with dons and poets. On New Year's Eve, when the hour of a quarter to twelve strikes, the heiroglyphicals of Magdalen cloisters descend and discuss together all that has been done in college during the past year. Oxford's carvings even have their own degree-giving ceremony, which takes place on Midsummer's Night in New College cloisters. In 1886, so it is said, the figures from the St. Swithun's building were (justly) awarded firsts and the elephant on the weathervane of the Indian Institute received a Doctorate of Common Law. Certain upstart and unimaginatively carved demons, excluded from the ceremony, made a dastardly attempt to lock the participants permanently in, so causing chaos in the city, especially as its bells were also there on brief leave. The moon, however, let down a ladder of moonbeams, by means of which they all escaped and returned to their accustomed places.

There they wait, ready to do your bidding: to astonish, to amuse, to instruct or to protect from harm. They reveal ambiguities, they hint at mysteries. Spontaneously free, they remind this learned city that effort and study must be balanced by humour and relaxation. They bring the past into the present and are an indispensible part of Oxford's being. As long as she endures, they will continue to lead their prominent yet secret lives.

3

2

2 The African influence on this New College Lane head is clear. The Pitt Rivers Museum contains marvellously strange and beautiful masks from all parts of the world. Anyone intending to practice the art of the grotesque would do well to visit them.

3 Pre-eminent among them stands this forty foot high totem pole from British Columbia.

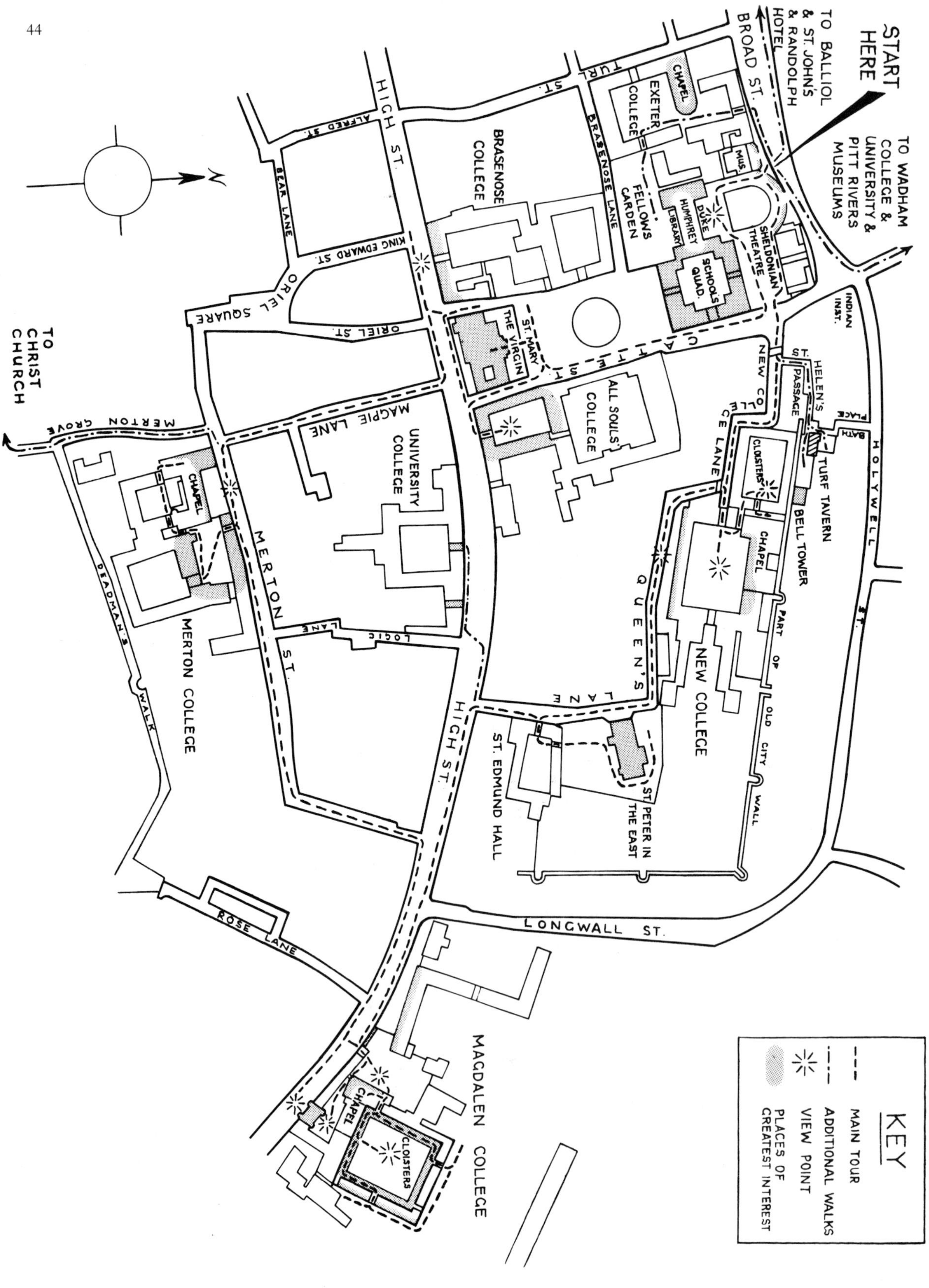

START HERE

TO WADHAM COLLEGE & UNIVERSITY & PITT RIVERS MUSEUMS

TO BALLIOL & ST. JOHN'S & RANDOLPH HOTEL

BROAD ST.

TURL ST.

HIGH ST.

ALFRED ST.

BEAR LANE

KING EDWARD ST.

ORIEL SQUARE

ORIEL ST.

EXETER COLLEGE

CHAPEL

MUS.

FELLOWS GARDEN

HUMPHREY LIBRARY

DUKE

SCHOOLS QUAD.

SHELDONIAN THEATRE

BRASENOSE COLLEGE

BRASENOSE LANE

ST. MARY THE VIRGIN

ALL SOULS' COLLEGE

NEW COLLEGE LANE

INDIAN INST.

ST. HELEN'S PASSAGE

TURF TAVERN

BATH PLACE

HOLYWELL ST.

CLOISTERS

BELL TOWER

CHAPEL

PART OF OLD CITY WALL

NEW COLLEGE

MAGPIE LANE

UNIVERSITY COLLEGE

MERTON GROVE

TO CHRIST CHURCH

N

CHAPEL

MERTON COLLEGE

DEADMAN'S WALK

MERTON ST.

LOGIC LANE

QUEEN'S LANE

ST. EDMUND HALL

ST. PETER IN THE EAST

HIGH ST.

LONGWALL ST.

ROSE LANE

CLOISTERS

CHAPEL

MAGDALEN COLLEGE

KEY

MAIN TOUR

ADDITIONAL WALKS

VIEW POINT

PLACES OF GREATEST INTEREST

PRINTED AT THE CRANHAM PRESS, JERICHO, OXFORD.